"Capitaine, voyage ton flag"
The Traditional Cajun Country Mardi Gras

Text by
Barry Jean Ancelet

Photo essay by
James Edmunds

The Center for Louisiana Studies
University of Southwestern Louisiana
Lafayette, Louisiana

ISBN Number: 0-940984-46-6

Copyright 1989
University of Southwestern Louisiana
Lafayette, Louisiana

Published by The Center for Louisiana Studies
University of Southwestern Louisiana

Introduction

Though not "sanctioned" by Rome, Mardi Gras is a popular traditional festival in many parts of the world, occurring on the last day before the beginning of the Lenten season. Mardi Gras, also called Carnival, has roots in the springtime rituals of the ancients and in medieval European adaptations of these practices. Survivals of these characteristics are still evident in contemporary celebrations of the Mardi Gras in the prairies of southwest Louisiana.

A key element of the Mardi Gras involves its roots in ancient springtime fertility rituals. These often functioned as a rite of passage for boys and girls by allowing them to act as men and women. This was sometimes accomplished by performing arduous tasks associated with manhood or womanhood, often involving surviving alone. It was sometimes of a more explicitly sexual nature. This aspect of the celebration can still be clearly seen in such manifestations as the Rio de Janeiro carnival, long based on the pursuit and realization of erotic fantasies. Even in the comparatively tame New Orleans Mardi Gras, one can see women baring their breasts for the crowds from their French Quarter balconies. Additionally the whip, part fertility symbol associated with such rituals since ancient civilizations and part instrument of intimidation, is frequently encountered in symbolic form during Mardi Gras celebrations. The black Mardi Gras streetwalkers in Lafayette, for example, often carry crepe paper whips. A remarkable survival of this fertility symbolism can be found in the women's Mardi Gras at Petit Mamou near Iota, where women collect ingredients for a communal gumbo just like the men. After the ride, however, the women sit on the floor in a circle singing their own version of the Mardi Gras song while a corresponding number of men dance around them pretending to whip them with symbolic whips made of braided burlap sacks.

The Mardi Gras is also based on a reversal of the social order, where supposed chaos rules. The king of the Rio Mardi Gras, for example, is Re Bobo, the King of Fools, or the King of Misrule. As early as medieval Europe, festivals of this sort have been associated with the Mardi Gras. The French chose *le Roi des Fous*. The English chose the Boy Bishop. In each case, the point of the celebration was to reverse the social order, to allow the lower classes to parody the upper classes. Men dressed as women, women as men. The poor dressed as rich, the rich as poor. The old dressed as young, the young as old. Black dressed as white, white as black. Within this ritual chaos, however, was a strict rules system without which such potentially threatening play was impossible. The ritual fool, or clown, was an important character in the celebration of Mardi Gras. The French clown was sometimes called *le paillasse,* or strawman, and could be identified by his clothes which were stuffed with straw.

A third key element of the Mardi Gras is its processional nature which has roots in African as well as European tradition. Unlike other traditional festivals which occur in a fixed place, the Mardi Gras moves about through the landscape, taking its celebration to people, sometimes whether they like it or not. The Mardi Gras processions move through towns and countryside alike invading public spaces like roads, rendering them impassible, and commercial districts, rendering them inoperable. Banks and merchants are forced to close for the madness.

A fourth element of the Mardi Gras is anonymity. Masks provide an opportunity to shed inhibitions and to take on roles for the day. Otherwise serious people can be transformed into clowns and otherwise timid people can become leaders. The altering of facial features, by means of masks or face painting, has long been associated with rites of passage for similar reasons.

A fifth element is related to the masking feature and involves the ritual altering of the consciousness. In some cultures, such as in South America and Africa, poisonous plants were ingested to cause delirious dreams for their rites of passage. Members of some American Indian tribes allow themselves to be bitten by poisonous snakes or scorpions to achieve delirium. Others smoked marijuana or peyote to the same effect. In European cultures, the ritual consumption of alcohol has long been a traditional way of altering the consciousness of celebrants.

Thus, far from being a mindless and masked drunken frenzy, the Mardi Gras provides a quite serious context for symbolic expressive behavior. Traditionally, as young boys become young men and young girls become young women, they shed their adolescence by stepping outside of themselves and imitating their elders in public, yet in secret. In this process, the ritual consumption of alcohol serves to loosen inhibitions, while the mask serves as a sort of cocoon, providing a cover for the changes occuring in the real self underneath.

La Course du Mardi Gras

The country Mardi Gras celebration of South Louisiana differs from its carnival counterparts in New Orleans and Lafayette. Like them, it is a processional festivity, but unlike them, it stems from the medieval *fête de la quémande*, a ceremonial begging tradition, with additional influences from the frontier heritage of the Louisiana prairies.

The *fête de la quémande* was celebrated by a procession of revelers who travelled through the countryside offering some sort of performance in exchange for gifts. Several modern celebrations are vestiges from this same source: costumed children making threats of trick or treat on Halloween, Christmas carolers singing for cups of hot chocolate or hot toddies, the chivari group making noise outside a neighbor's house until invited in for food or drink, Irish mummers performing impromptu plays from house to house in exchange for a drink during the Christmas season. Other Franco-American ceremonial begging traditions associated with Mardi Gras and Lent are *La Guignollée* in Missouri and *la Mi-Carême* in Quebec. The Mardi Gras Indian tradition in New Orleans is also similar in that bands of masked and costumed men go from bar to bar on Mardi Gras day singing and dancing with the expectation of being invited in for a drink. Some notable New Orleans music stems from this tradition, including such songs as "Iko Iko" and "Me Big Chief." Similarly, during the *course de Mardi Gras*, on the southwestern Louisiana prairies, a band of masked riders visit their neighbors in the country side around little towns, singing and dancing to the traditional Mardi Gras song (which has its origins in medieval modal music), at each that will receive them. The goal of these performances is a contribution to their communal gumbo shared later that day. Sometimes this is a bag of flour, or rice, a sack of onions or even money, but ideally it is a live chicken which the participants are expected to catch themselves.

Reinforcing its medieval origins, the traditional costumes for the course have roots in medieval dress. In additional to the unavoidable modern clowns, monsters, and cartoon characters are the conical hats (in parody of noble women and also long associated with dunces or fools), mitres (in parody of the clergy), and more rarely, mortarboards (in parody of scholars and clerics). False collars and brightly colored costumes often in harlequin sequences add to the medieval flavor. Masks sometimes preserve ancient parodies, reversing sexual and racial roles, casting humans as animals, and other traditional masking devices. Other times masks can represent contemporary parodies, reflecting current political and economic realities as well as media-driven preoccupations.

A certain medieval atmosphere is enhanced by the processional nature of the Mardi Gras celebration. Instead of taking place in a fixed location, like a festival, it moves through the countryside. Moreover, musicians who accompany the ride in a closed wagon following the riders evoke images of the jesters of the Middle Ages whose only role was to provide entertainment for the court, and just as the jester never really participated directly in the festivities for which he provided entertainment, the Mardi Gras musicians remain marginal figures, never coming out of their wagon to take part in the activities of the riders.

Other medieval survivals have been identified in Kinder's version of the Mardi Gras. There most participants walk the entire way, frequently pretending to flog each other with rolled burlap sacks, reminiscent of the processions of the flagellators who sought to atone for the sins of their society during the plagues of the Middle Ages. There also, brief spontaneous plays are sometimes performed, including "The Dead Man Revived," once popular among the miracle players on the steps of medieval cathedrals. In this pre-Arthurian play, one participant feigns death and his companions "revive" him by dropping wine or beer into his mouth. An analogy to this traditional element can also be found in ancient drinking songs, like "*Chevaliers de la table ronde*," and "*Fais trois tours de la table ronde*."

In addition to its medieval begging celebration origins, the *course de Mardi Gras* is also characterized by a mystique of toughness reminiscent of the days of the American Wild West. The anonymity of the masked riders provided an ideal reckoning ground for quarreling parties. In earlier times scores were often settled on this day with bare fists, knives and even pistols. Additionally, groups of riders, overwhelmed by the festival spirit, mildly terrorized many visited households, forcing women to dance, sometimes vandalizing property, whether intentionally or accidentally. While the main party distracted the hosts in the front yard, riders sometimes strayed to the back of the house to steal from the kitchen.

Throughout the nineteenth century and even into the early part of the twentieth century, the *course de Mardi Gras* could be found in most areas of French Louisiana from the Mississippi River to the Texas border. With the arrival of Americanization and the "civilizing" effect of new schools and churches, however, the often rowdy celebration was banned from many communities and eventually disappeared from the annual cycle of Louisiana

French folklife. In the early 1950s, a group of cultural activists in the Mamou area, under the leadership of Paul Tate and Revon Reed, undertook to revive the traditional Mardi Gras run. They sought guidance from older members of the community, notably from Lezime Fontenot, "Petit Nan" Augustine, and Marcellus Deshotels, who remembered running Mardi Gras and even remembered the words of that community's version of the traditional Mardi Gras song which itself describes the nature of the celebration.

La Chanson de Mardi Gras

Capitaine, Capitaine, voyage ton *flag*.
Allons se mettre dessus le chemin.
Capitaine, Capitaine, voyage ton *flag*.
Allons aller chez l'autre voisin.

Les Mardi Gras se rassemblent une fois par an
Pour demander la charité.
Ça va aller de porte en porte
Tout à l'entour du moyeu.

Les Mardi Gras viennent de tout partout,
Ouais, mon cher bon camarade.
Les Mardi Gras viennent de tout partout,
Mais tout à l'entour du moyeu.

Les Mardi Gras viennent de tout partout,
Mais principalement de Grand Mamou.
Les Mardi Gras viennent de tout partout,
Tout à l'entour du moyeu.

Voulez-vous recevoir
Mais cette bande de Mardi Gras?
Voulez-vous recevoir
Mais cette bande de grands saoulards?

Les Mardi Gras demandent la rentrée
Au maître et la maîtresse.
Ça demande la rentrée
Avec toutes les politesses.

Donnez-nous autres une petite poule grasse
Pourqu'on se fasse un gumbo gras.
Donnez-nous autres une petite poule grasse
Tout à l'entour du moyeu.

Donnez-nous autres un peu de la graisse,
S'il vous plaît, mon caramie.
Donnez-nous autres un peu de riz,
Tout à l'entour, mon ami.

Les Mardi Gras vous remercient bien
Pour votre bonne volonté.
Les Mardi Gras vous remercient bien
Pour votre bonne volonté.

On vous invite tous pour le bal à soir,
Là-bas à Grand Mamou.
On vous invite tous pour le gros bal,
Tout à l'entour du moyeu.

On vous invite tous pour le gros gombo
Là-bas à la cuisine.
On vous invite tous pour le gros gombo
Là-bas chez John Vidrine.

Capitaine, Capitaine, voyage ton *flag*.
Allons se mettre dessus le chemin.
Capitaine, Capitaine, voyage ton *flag*.
Allons aller chez l'autre voisin.

(Traditional; as sung by Elby Deshotels; recorded by Harry Oster)

In reviving the tradition, Tate and Reed took great pains to render the celebration respectable and relatively safe for both riders and hosts, without emasculating the rite of passage. This effort, anchored in the absolute control of the *capitaine*, encouraged the continuation of the course by virtually eliminating fights and the element of danger. There is, however, an interesting tension between begging and demanding which persists even today. Riders await permission to approach a house, then charge it as though taking it by storm. They then sing and dance for an offering, then chase the chicken through the barnyard as though stealing it. Riders play at changing roles from beggar to outlaw, singing and dancing while intimidating non-participants.

This celebration has since been revived in several area towns, including Church Point, Eunice, Basile, and L'Anse Meg. There are now even a few *courses* for women only, such as in Petit Mamou, near Iota, and Basile, both in Evangeline Parish. Mixture of both sexes was common long ago, but now it is extremenly rare. Ironically, the "males only" restriction is said to have originated among the women of Mamou who intended to reduce the possibility of anonymous carousing among their men. Most other towns followed suit in reviving their versions of the celebration. Among these riders, there exists the same sorts of sexual freedoms that one encounters in other exclusively male groups such as sports teams or campers. For this occasion, men do things that they would not ordinarily do in mixed company, such as dance together, walk arm-in-arm, and embrace each other. In fact, a popular costume motif involves the reversal of sexual identity by wearing wigs, dresses and even false bosoms. This kind of activity happens frequently among men who have no doubts about their own identities. The toughest men can afford to play at being feminine without arousing any suspicions concerning their sexuality.

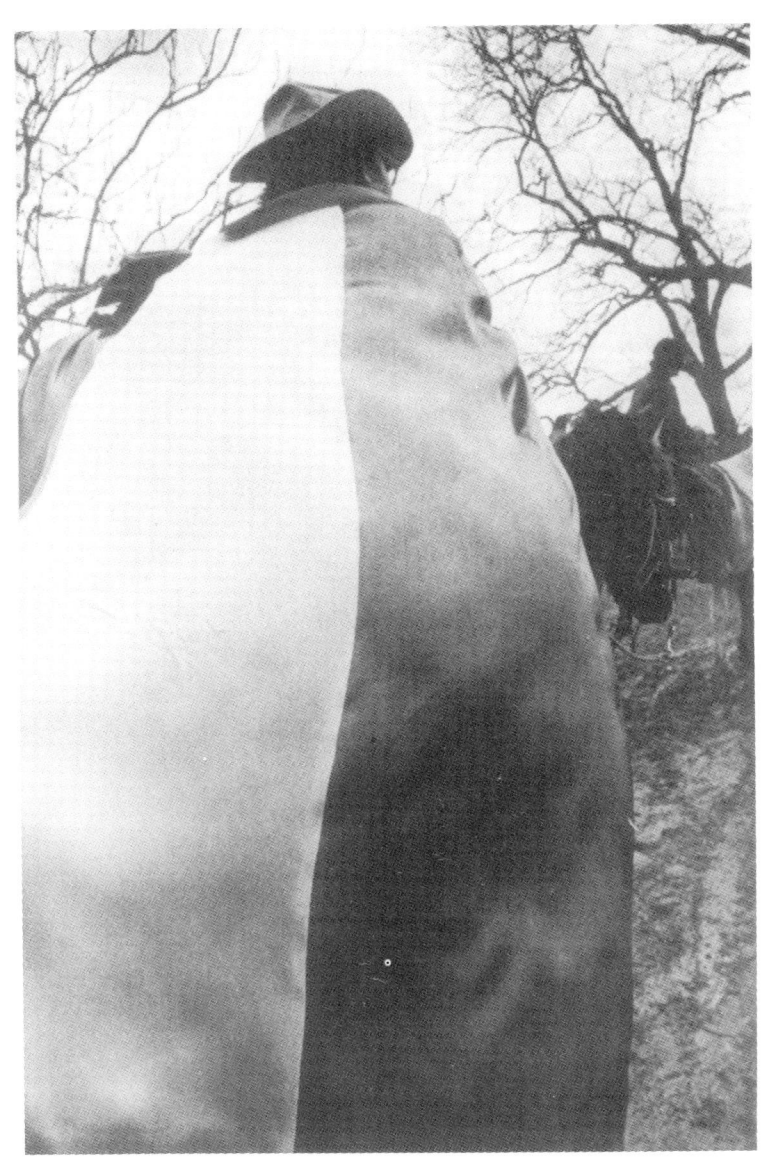

Capitaine, Capitaine, voyage ton *flag*.
Allons se mettre dessus le chemin.
Capitaine, Capitaine, voyage ton *flag*.
Allons aller chez l'autre voisin.

Les Mardi Gras se rassemblent une fois par an
Pour demander la charité.
Ça va aller de porte en porte
Tout à l'entour du moyeu.

Les Mardi Gras viennent de tout partout,
Ouais, mon cher bon camarade.

Les Mardi Gras viennent de tout partout,
Mais tout à l'entour du moyeu.

Voulez-vous recevoir
Mais cette bande de Mardi Gras?
Voulez-vous recevoir
Mais cette bande de grands saoulards?

Les Mardi Gras demandent la rentrée
Au maître et la maîtresse.
Ça demande la rentrée
Avec toutes les politesses.

Donnez-nous autres une petite poule grasse
Pourqu'on se faise un gumbo gras.
Donnez-nous autres une petite poule grasse
Tout à l'entour du moyeu.

Donnez-nous autres un peu de la graisse,
S'il vous plaît, mon caramie.

Donnez-nous autres un peu de riz,
Tout à l'entour, mon ami.

Les Mardi Gras vous remercient bien
Pour votre bonne volonté.

Les Mardi Gras vous remercient bien
Pour votre bonne volonté.

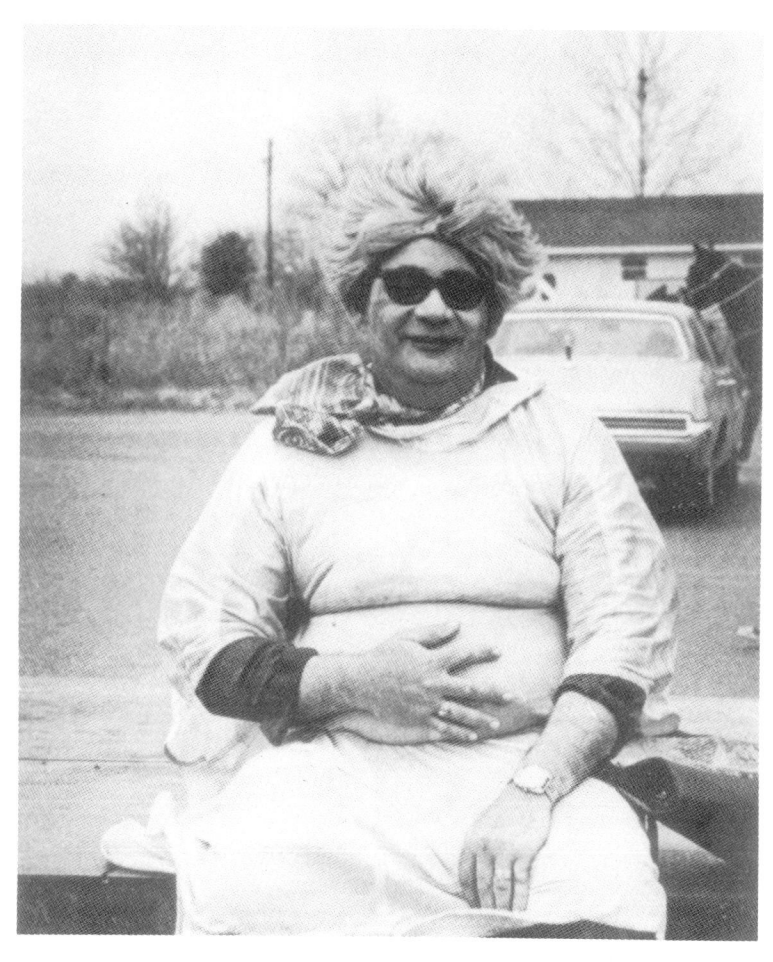

On vous invite tous pour le bal à soir,
Là-bas à Grand Mamou.

On vous invite tous pour le gros bal,
Tout à l'entour du moyeu.

On vous invite tous pour le gros gombo
Là-bas à la cuisine.

On vous invite tous pour le gros gombo
Là-bas chez John Vidrine.

Capitaine, Capitaine, voyage ton *flag*.
Allons se mettre dessus le chemin.
Capitaine, Capitaine, voyage ton *flag*.
Allons aller chez l'autre voisin.

The Mamou version of the celebration by virtue of its precedence and of its deliberate sense of tradition, provides an ideal model for understanding the structure of the country Mardi Gras. A certain aura of outlawry has not entirely vanished from the modern version of the celebration in Mamou, which effectively resists transformation into a simple tourist attraction by its sheer toughness. In fact, the celebration, strictly limited to male participation, is sufficiently exacting to be a functional rite of passage for the young men of the community. Reminiscent of the rite of passage in primitive societies, the social initiation on the morning of the ride is accentuated by solitude and anonymity, and all inhibitions being removed, the initiate passes through the essential part of the ordeal: being all he dares to be. Except for the list of rules imposed by the game itself, there is virtually no limit to the personal freedom of expression available to the rider.

Participation in the Mamou Mardi Gras can begin several weeks in advance with a series of informal meetings to determine certain administrative roles for the event, such as beer truck personnel, tractor drivers (to pull wagons for those without horses), and musicians, all of whom will not actually run in the Mardi Gras. The *capitaine,* named for life by his predecessor, chooses his co-*capitaines* who will assist him during the ride. Just as in the American West, often the toughest and hardest to control become co-*capitaines,* thereby channeling their energies in the right direction. There are no elections; the Mardi Gras Riders Association makes no concessions to democracy. Brief business meetings quickly become rallies, building excitement for the coming ride.

On the eve of the celebration, riders make final preparations for the course. These preparations are often complicated by the fact that many riders handle horses once a year, on Mardi Gras. Moreover, many riders, to avoid recognition, exchange horses several times before Mardi Gras day, and since many local riders are in the habit of playing practical jokes, or *niches,* on one-another, it is not uncommon on the morning of the ride to find one's horse with all the tail hairs pulled out or some other sort of mischief.

After settling on a plan for the next day, riders usually convene informally on the eve of the ride in a local bar for some pre-celebration festivities. For the past several years, Revon Reed has presented an excerpt from "*Dedans le sud de la Louisiane,*" a documentary film of a previous Mamou Mardi Gras by French filmmaker Jean-Pierre Brunot, in Fred's Lounge that evening, and most of the men in effect see themselves engaged in the activities that they are so eagerly awaiting the following day. As they watch themselves charging farmhouses on command from the *capitaine*, dancing wildly, singing, drinking and chasing chickens, emotions soar until the audience is in a frenzy of anticipation. A festive spirit is maintained throughout the evening with the driving sounds of live Cajun music played spontaneously by a number of local musicians. As one might expect, the Mardi Gras figures prominently in the repertoire of the evening. What happens, then, resembles closely the ancient tradition of telling war stories or singing epics of adventure to rally the troops the night before a battle.

At dawn the next morning, riders don their costumes and masks, saddle their horses and start down the country roads and back streets to join their fellows. Arriving at the appointed gathering place, the local American Legion Hall, the brilliantly arrayed riders mill around, usually somewhat slowly because of the revelry of the previous evening. Most riders know one-another but, for a while at least, they recognize few. As time passes, the area becomes filled with rowdy, masked horsemen. At a certain point the *capitaine* requests that the riders gather inside the hall for the reading of the rules. The *capitaine* and his co-*capitaines* are unmasked so that they may represent the band of revelers to each household they visit. They are further identified by their cowboy hats and long multi-colored capes, usually a two-colored combination of purple, yellow, red and green. From the time he takes command of the celebration at the reading of the rules to the restrained and relatively orderly re-entry into town later in the day, the *capitaine*'s reign is absolute. This is a result of a tacit agreement among all riders who play the game. For an entire day, a considerable number of adult males willingly suspend reality for the sake of the ritual celebration, the nature of which demands unquestioning submission to the authority of a chosen leader whose role is to act as intermediary between the madness of the procession and the outside world they will visit.

The rules are read first in French then in English by the *capitaine* who stands on a chair to address the riders, called Mardi Gras. The rules are designed to maintain a firm structural framework for the festivities. Some are preventative: no Mardi Gras shall advance beyond the *capitaine* on the route; no Mardi Gras shall enter private property without the explicit permission of the *capitaine;* no Mardi Gras shall consume any liquor except that which is distributed by the *capitaine* and his assistants; no Mardi Gras shall bear arms or weapons of any kind, including knives, guns or sticks. Others are meant to keep the tradition intact: no Mardi Gras shall throw beads, doubloons or trinkets of any sort anywhere along the route; all Mardi

Gras are expected to dismount from horses and wagons to sing and dance at the homes which give an offering for the gumbo.

At the end of the English translation of the rules, the riders file through the only unlocked door to be thoroughly frisked. This is as much to prevent women from infiltrating the ride as to enforce the no weapons rule. The age limit of eighteen is sometimes mitigated by circumstances like the company of a guardian or a judgement of maturity. Riders then mount their steeds and unmounted troops mount the wagons. The procession then leaves town to the tune of the Mardi Gras song, which will be played again dozens of times during the day, and proceeds under the strict leadership of the *capitaine* and his assistants on a predetermined but secret route.

As the procession approaches the first house, the tension of the previous evening begins to mount in anticipation of the traditional charge. The *capitaine* halts the band of riders on the road and rides ahead alone with raised white flag to ask the residents' permission to enter, according to custom. If permission is granted, he drops his flag to signal the invitation to charge the house.

Surrounding the front yard, the riders dismount and begin singing and dancing to the Mardi Gras, played on each visit by the live musicians who accompany the ride in their own wagon. Previously all riders were required to know at least a few verses of the Mardi Gras song and they sang it themselves during the course of the day. In recent years, this tradition has faded somewhat, and the ritual performance of the song has become the responsibility of the musicians. Some of the more daring riders might playfully snatch up the lady of the house and her daughters and dance with them in the crowd. Children are often the object of some mock terrorism by the masked riders, sometimes being whisked away from their parents for a brief moment in an unsolicited lesson in being away from the safety of home and family.

After an appropriate amount of revelry, the man of the house brings out an offering for the Mardi Gras. This may be flour, rice, onions, oil, or money. Ideally, however, it is a live chicken which he throws high in the air. Those closest to it chase it down and the captor jubilantly holds up his prize for all to see before surrendering it to one of the co-*capitaines* who will place it in a cage until it can be transported back to town to find its way into the gumbo. After a bit more dancing and socializing, the *capitaine* blows his cow horn to call the riders to order and the procession moves on to the next house.

At regular intervals between houses, the *capitaine* calls a halt to the procession for a beer stop. A pickup truck loaded with beer parks in the middle of the road and the riders file by to receive their ration of beer under the scrutiny of the co-*capitaines*. The fact that alcohol consumption is controlled does not mean that it is not liberal. Many riders have ample opportunity to work themselves into a state of ritual inebriation. This aspect of the Mardi Gras, when viewed out of context, can make the celebration appear reckless and unkempt. Yet it can appear less offensive when viewed from the perspective of history and tradition in terms of the ancient tradition of altered consciousness long associated with such rituals.

Sometimes, especially during these beer stops, a rider might wander out in front of the group past the *capitaine* only to be briskly reminded of the rule requiring all riders to stay behind the *capitaine* at all times. Errors are corrected sheepishly; no one challenges the authority of the *capitaine*.

While the riders show complete respect for the *capitaine*, they show considerably less for everyone else. There are always countless photographers, journalists, ethnographers, and other such "foreigners" accompanying the ride and, often enough, an over-zealous documenter will get in the way of a group of riders. Patience with this interference soon wears thin and more than one visitor has found himself surrounded by taunting riders, pushed into a roadside ditch or even stung by the flick of a riding crop. Ordinarily, the *capitaine* deftly disregards these activities, owing allegiance to the ride itself and not to those who would witness it from outside. The Mamou Mardi Gras, by far the most heavily documented of the courses, has ironically also been among the most successful in resisting the media and tourists. Long-time *capitaine* Jasper Manuel answered requests for hand signals to the next house from media personnel with a casual, "If I think about it, but as you can imagine, I've got a lot of other things on my mind." He usually remembered for a house or two, then somehow forgot, often just before a turn which effectively pinned the front-runners at the corner until the procession was safely past. On the Church Point run of 1979, an ABC television crew filming a segment for the program 20/20 somehow succeeded in having a charge repeated because they missed it the first time. During this repeat performance, several horses fell and at least one rider received minor injuries. Since then, the *capitaine* has tended to ignore such requests from the media.

Horses and riders are invariably weary and ragged as they approach the edge of town at the end of the long ride in mid-afternoon. The *capitaine* orders a stop just inside the city limits for the riders to regroup, repair tack and costumes, and regain a certain composure for the grand, triumphant reentry into town. Riders present themselves as surviving warriors to those townsfolk who did not participate in the ordeal. With a strong sense of brotherhood based on their shared experiences, they parade down the length of the crowded main street in haughty silence, once again to the tune of the Mardi Gras song, deigning now and then to wave in victory to the spectators along the way. Finally, the band of Cajun musicians who have been performing for a street dance in town (designed by run organizers to keep as many visitors as possible in town) give the stage to the Mardi Gras musicians for a grand performance of the Mardi Gras song, which can last up to half an hour, while the riders dance in the crowd. Most riders then retire to a quiet spot to await their hard-earned supper, the ceremonial gumbo, made with chickens caught along the way. Now the gumbo must be stretched with chickens from the market to feed the growing multitudes of visitors. Riders eat first. Some go home to rest or take their horses back to the barn before returning later for the masked ball which marks the final hours of this final fling of revelry before the beginning of Lent the next day on Ash Wednesday. All festivities stop abruptly at midnight and many of Tuesday's rowdiest riders can be found on their knees receiving ashes on their foreheads on Wednesday.